Strasbourg

**Walks thr...
and t...**

Strasbourg around 1850

Text: Marie-Christine Périllon; Photographs: Airdiasol/Rothan

Kraichgau Verlag

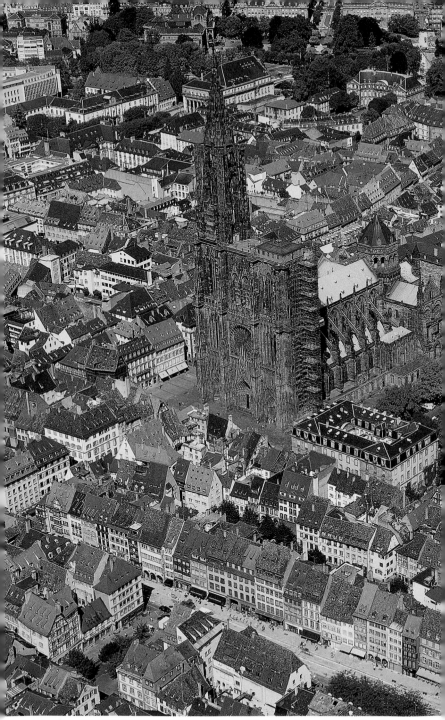

A city with 276,000 inhabitants whose historical centre nestles between

the arms of the river Ill, a tributary of the Rhine.

Welcome to Strasbourg

Right at the beginning we should mention that - thanks to the European TGV - Strasbourg is only 2 hours and 20 minutes from Paris and it will become

the pivot of European high-speed rail traffic.

Strasbourg is also a city that should be visited on foot. The city centre, the "grande île" or "large island" – classed, like Venice or Prague, as a UNESCO world heritage site – was established between the arms of the river Ill. In fact, the splitting of this tributary of the Rhine creates an elliptical island on which is found the entire historical centre of the city, from the first Roman settlement to the elegant 18th century houses. This large island is nevertheless small enough to be crossed on foot in a quarter of an hour or less, depending on the pace and the chosen route. An astonishing concentration of architectural masterpieces is assembled within its 83 hectares. Among them are the cathedral, the Ponts Couverts (covered bridges), the Palais Rohan and many other buildings bearing

striking witness to the civil and religious life of a city which is more than 2000 years old. It is therefore best to leave the car in one of the numerous car-parks around the periphery of the city and either continue from there on foot, let the large transparent tram take you through the city as if you were on a moving walkway, or hire a bicycle. There are fixed prices – car-park + tram, car-park + bicycle hire – which make this a very comfortable solution. Only the European quarter and the "ville allemande" (German town), which are further out of the centre, require extra transport.

The various architectural styles in the city prompted Le Corbusier to say that in Strasbourg "the eye is never bored". This is just as true with regard to Strasbourg's cultural and gastronomic offerings.

It is impossible to become bored in a city whose cultural budget is second only to that of Paris. An opera house, twenty or so theatres, including the only Théâtre National outside Paris, nine museums, café-theatres, jazz clubs and new music venues, not forgetting the European centre for young creativity, based in a former dairy: all these contribute to the rich cultural palette offered by Strasbourg. Festivals like Musica, devoted to contemporary music, or the Festival International de Musique, more classical, have gained a reputation across Europe. In the summer a great open-air event, concerts, poetic soirees, illuminations at the

cathedral are all part of an extremely varied programme of free entertainment which is enjoyed by locals and tourists alike. What is more, the latter can benefit all year round from the "Strasbourg Pass", valid for three days, which offers numerous discounts for events taking place throughout the year. Finally, it is impossible to round off without referring to the gastronomic pleasures of a city with wine bars and Michelin-starred restaurants in abundance.

A visit to one of these picturesquely-named establishments remains the best introduction to discovering Strasbourg.

5

Chronology

12 B.C.:	Installation of a Roman settlement on the site of Argentoratum.
70 A.D.:	Arrival of Augustus' 8th legion in Argentoratum.
451:	Having endured Alemannic invasions, Argentoratum is devasted by Attila's Huns.
496:	Clovis definitively beats the Alemanni at Tolbiac and thus claims Argentoratum for Francia. Argentoratum becomes Strateburgum, "the city of roads".
842:	The grandsons of Charlemagne, Louis the German and Charles the Bald, exchange the famous Serments de Strasbourg, the first written evidence of the Romance and Teutonic languages, and thus split the Carolingian kingdom between them.
870:	Through the Treaty of Meersen Louis the German obtains Alsace, which he integrates into the Germanic Holy Roman Empire.
974:	The episcopal authority, which rules the city, obtains permission to mint its own currency.
1176:	Beginning of construction of the current cathedral.
1201:	Strasbourg has its own seal: a Virgin with outstretched arms.
1262:	The artisans take over power after beating the episcopal troops at the Battle of Hausbergen.
1332:	Taking advantage of the quarrel between the Zorns and the Müllenheims – two noble families of the city – the artisans create a council, elected from within their number, with its seat in Ammeister.
1349:	Political troubles due to the Black Plague and the massacre of the Jews.
1439:	The cathedral's spire is completed.
1482:	Final alterations to Strasbourg's Constitution, which will remain unchanged until the Revolution.
1518:	Luther's 95 theses mark the beginning of the Reformation.
1529:	The Assembly of Aldermen votes to recognise the Reformation.

1549-1559:	An interim of 10 years is imposed by Charles Quint: the cathedral reverts to Catholicism.
1604:	Treaty of Haguenau: the bishopric war ends in victory for the Catholic representative, Charles de Lorraine.
1621:	The Haute Ecole, founded by Jean Sturm in 1538, attains the rank of a university.
1681:	As an indirect consequence of the Treaties of Westphalia, Strasbourg goes back to French rule under Louis XIV.
1721:	Charles-François Hannong founds Strasbourg's ceramics manufactory.
1744:	Louis XV receives an impressive welcome on his visit to Strasbourg.
21st July 1789:	Strasbourg's town hall is pillaged following the announcement of the storming of the Bastille.
1790:	De Dietrich becomes mayor of Strasbourg. It is in his rooms in place Broglie on 26th April 1792 that the hymn which will become the Marseillaise is sung for the first time.

1806-1808:	Napoleon and Josephine stay in Strasbourg.

1836: Napoleon III fails to rouse the Strasbourg garrison into restoring the empire.

1870: Siege of Strasbourg and surrender to the German empire.

1871: Strasbourg becomes capital of the Reichsland of Alsace-Lorraine.

1918: After the abdication of William II a soviet of soldiers and workers takes over in Strasbourg from 10th November until the arrival on 22nd November of French troops under the leadership of General Gouraud.

1939: In the face of impending war, the population of Strasbourg is evacuated to south-west France.

1940: On 18th June German troops enter Strasbourg. Alsace is annexed to Germany and the refugees return.

23rd November 1944: Liberation of Strasbourg by the troops of General Leclerc.

1949: Foundation of the Council of Europe, which chooses Strasbourg as its base.

1979: First session of the European Parliament in Strasbourg, presided by Louise Weiss. Election of the Parliament by universal suffrage.

1992: During the Edinburgh Summit, Strasbourg is designated permanent seat of the European Parliament, which leads to the construction of a new chamber, completed in 1998.

Place de la Cathédrale ①

Place de la Cathédrale is a favourite starting place for tours. It is situated at Strasbourg's highest point – 144 metres. In the past markets selling cherries, bread and rags were held here on a daily basis. Today, the attraction of the square's grandiose monument ensures that it is still a place of perpetual activity.

But two other buildings deserve our particular attention. The first is the **Kammerzell house,** the largest and most decorated of all the half-timbered houses in Strasbourg. Its facade contains seventy-five windows whose sculpted frames depict different characters from the bible and from mythology, but also the

In the shadow of the cathedral stands the most attractive half-timbered house in Strasbourg: the Kammerzell house.

With its seventy-five windows framed by sculptures illustrating religious and secular themes, the Kammerzell house seems to want to rival the cathedral.

signs of the zodiac, the five senses and a series of musicians. On the corner posts the three Virtues are represented. At the first floor level, Charity is accompanied by two children and a pelican, while on the up-per floors Hope is represented by a phoenix and Faith by a griffin. In the 16th century a cheese merchant named Martin Braun acquired the house and completed its restoration in 1589. The only part left of the

On the corner post: the allegory of Charity.

◀ *Haus Kammerzell:*
The ground floor with mediaeval arches.

mediaeval building was the ground floor with its triple arch. The other storeys were reconstructed, making way for the splendid Renaissance construction we see today. It was known as the Altes Haus (old house) until the middle of the 19th century, when it became the property of a Würzburg grocer, Philippe-François Kammerzell, after whom the house was named. Inside are frescos by Léo Schnug (1878-1933), a painter who also decorated the castle Haut

Modern icons under the serious gaze of the prophets.

The former Pharmacie du Cerf. Today it houses the "Boutique Culture" (ticket sale for concerts, theatre plays, festivals, etc.)

Koenigsbourg, depicting the Ship of Fools and the Torment of Tantalus in the style of the Rhenish artists of the 16th century. The building, which today houses a restaurant, became municipal property in 1879 and was classed as a historical monument.

A little further, opposite the west portals of the cathedral, can be seen the former **Pharmacie du Cerf,** first cited in the 13th century. Its stone ground floor, whose arcades are decorated with branches and snakes, is from that period. The upper, half-timbered floors date from 1567, as attested by the date still visible on the sandstone column. This supporting column, which creates a gap between itself and the facade, is known as the "büchmesser", or "stomach measurer", according to a tradition relating to the stone-masons, who were required to remain below a certain level of corpulence, so as to be able to slip into the crevices in the cathedral.

13

The cathedral ②

"It is a giant and delicate marvel": the cathedral does indeed match Victor Hugo's definition, with its 142-metre spire and its appearance of lace-like stone. The building stands on the foundations of a former Romanesque basilica constructed in 1015 by Bishop Wernher of the Hapsburg family. Destroyed by fire, it was replaced by a new cathedral. Nearly four centuries passed between the starting of the

foundations in 1176 to the completion of the spire in 1439. Its height made Strasbourg's Notre-Dame the highest building in Christendom until the 19th century, when it was overtaken by the towers in Ulm and Cologne.

Part of the crypt and the apse are vestiges of the earlier basilica built by Wernher in Romanesque style. In around 1225, the arrival of a team from Chartres revolutionised the course of the construction. A master builder whose name has not been passed down to us introduced the local craftsmen to the splendours of Gothic art, which had up to then been ignored. He was responsible for masterpieces such as the Pillar of Angels and the statues of Church and Synagogue (transept and south portal).

Embedded in the heart of the old city, a cathedral always surrounded by much activity.

The principal facade

The west side was started towards 1270. One of its interesting features can be seen in the stencilled arcades mounted in front of the supporting walls, which give a lace-like impression. Art historians have described this as "harpes de pierre" or stone harpstrings.

The tympana of the three portals are dedicated to the life of Christ and to the last judgement. On the jambs of the right portal the group, doubtless the best known, consists of the Tempter and the Wise and Foolish Virgins. On the left portal the Virtues elegantly overwhelm the Vices.

An astonishingly delicate double gable surmounts each portal. In the centre, surrounded by sixteen finely

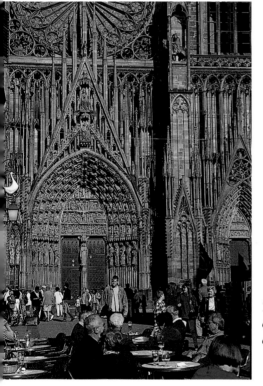

The portals of the facade are encased by "harpes de pierre" or stone harpstrings.

Cathedral opening times: every day 7.00am – 11.20am and 12.35pm – 7.00pm. Astronomical Clock: every day at 12.30pm. Entry through the south portal from 11.20pm. Ticket Office opens at 11.50am. Film projection on astronomical clock: every day at 12pm. It is possible to climb the tower (332 steps).

Notre-Dame, Strasbourg, characterised by its single tower, whose spire reaches a height of 142 metres. Goethe liked to greet the sunset from its high platform.

The main portal relates the Passion of Christ with little grotesque details beloved of sculptors in the Middle Ages.

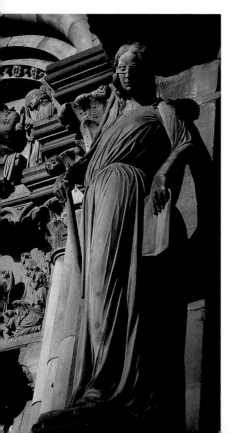

stencilled stone petals, blooms the rose window attributed to Erwin de Steinbach, master builder of the cathedral from 1284 to 1318. Above them, two towers linked by a belfry since the end of the 14th century form a platform to which one can climb for a marvellous panoramic view.

The Synagogue is depicted on the south portal.

At the second storey level, the six-petalled rose window created by
Erwin de Steinbach offers the allure of a jewel set in a costly ring.

19

The viewing platform

At this level the visitor has barely reached the halfway point of the edifice (66 m), in contrast to what he might be led to believe by the optical illusion created when looking down. From the platform rises

◀ A downward view from the height of the platform over the roofs of the city.

The edifice is crowned by ▶ a pyramid-shaped spire.

▼ The Kammerzell house seen from above.

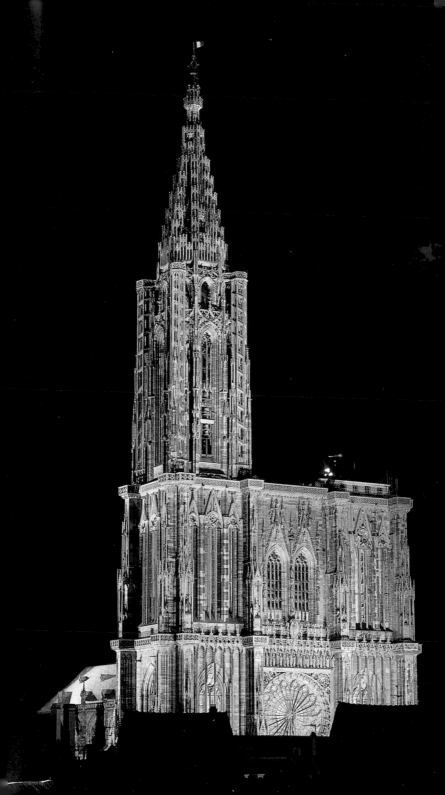

the octagonal tower constructed by Ulrich d'Ensingen before Jean Hultz took over to add the stencilled spire.

The spire consists of eight internal staircases leading to a turret crowned with a cross. The excursion to the extreme point of the spire was allowed until the last century and inspired several writers such as Goethe and Stendahl, who tell of it in their writings.

The side portals

On the south side of the cathedral the beautiful clock portal, with its still Romanesque styling the oldest of the cathedral, is flanked by statues representing Church and Synagogue. The tympanum of the left door is decorated with a beautiful illustration of the death of the Virgin, shown surrounded by the Apostles, who have come from all corners of the earth to accompany her on her final journey. There is a change in decoration on the north side of the cathedral, where the Magi portal is a good example of the realistic style towards the end of the Middle Ages, while the tympanum shows a portrayal of the martyring of St. Laurent.

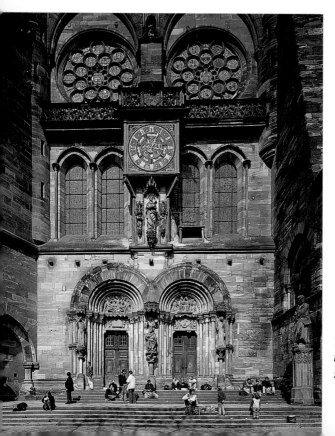

The Romanesque tympana on the south portals.

The interior

The nave (64 m long, 32 m high), inspired by thaat of the cathedral of Saint-Denis, was constructed in two stages between 1240 and 1275. On entering, the visitor is struck by the fact that most of the original stained glass windows have been preserved. Their golden brilliance is due to the bright colours preferred by the Strasbourg master glaziers. The oldest windows, from the 13th century, are to be found on the lower north side and represent a succession of emperors of the Ger-

The organ case with the famous "Rohraffe" or howler monkey.

manic Holy Roman Empire. The Virgin in the chancel, a gift from the Council of Europe in 1957, is a contemporary window by Max Ingrand. When it comes to furniture, the organ case from 1385, the most people during the religious services at Whitsun. Their mission was to denounce the excesses of the church which were typical of the period before the Reformation. A great preacher of the time took no

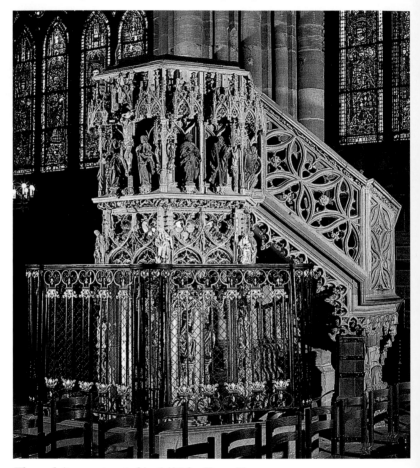

The pulpit, constructed in 1485 by Hans Hammer.

adorned with singular characters like the Rohraffe or howler monkey, never fails to attract attention. Throughout the Middle Ages these moving mannequins, given voice by a cleric hidden inside, attracted heed of this: the famous Geiler de Kaysersberg, for whom the flamboyant Gothic throne, still on view today, was constructed in 1485.

The nave is 32 metres high.

The transept

Under the north transept there still remains a supporting pillar from the Romanesque period. It is in this section of the building that the oldest windows can be found (end of the 12th, beginning of the 13th century). They show the two St. Johns, a judgement of Solomon and a small Virgin Mary originating from the first Romanesque sanctuary constructed on this site. Also from the Romanesque period is the sculpted frieze of fabulous characters which decorates the niche containing flamboyant Gothic baptismal fonts produced by Jost Dotzinger in 1453. The eye is drawn to a group sculpted in a very theatrical pose: a Mount of Olives scene from 1498, which was formerly on the graveyard of St. Thomas' church. Visitors who

The Mount of Olives, from 1498.

are pressed for time hurry towards the south transept, and rightly so, for everyone has heard of the famous astronomical clock, a marvel of science and technology. A product of

The chapel of St. John the Baptist.

The choir, under a Romanesque dome, has been modified several times.

27

The Pillar of Angels.

endar. Spectators are particularly drawn by the automated figures which, every day at 12.30pm, parade before Christ, who blesses them three times before blessing the crowd. Peter's denial of Christ is recalled by chanting and by the flapping of a cock's wings. There is another parade every quarter of an hour: the four stages of life parade in front of Death, while an angel turns a sandglass to mark the passing of each quarter of an hour. Finally, visitors should not miss the chance to admire the gods of Antiquity, who, from Mars to Venus, parade in their elegant chariots to symbolise the different days of the week.

Having satisfied his curiosity about the astronomical clock, the visitor may turn his full attention to the Pilier des Anges (Pillar of Angels), a representation of the Last Judgement dating from 1225-30, whose characters spiral delicately out of the stone in a most splendid announcement of the arrival of Gothic style in the cathedral. The various chapels are also to be recommended: St. André, the oldest, St. Jean for the tomb of Conrad de Lichtenberg and the epitaph of Nicolas Gerhaert de Leyde, St. Catherine for its 14th century stained glass windows, St. Laurent for its 18th century altar.

the Reformation, it was completed in around 1570 by the Strasbourg mathematician Conrad Dasypodius and a team of Swiss clock-makers. The clock was out of service from the time of the Revolution until it was given new life in 1842 by Jean-Baptiste Schwilgué, who added a model of the Copernican planetary system and an ecclesiastical cal-

The famous astronomical clock with its automated figures.

The Palais Rohan ③

From 1704 until the Revolution four cardinals of the Rohan family led the bishopric of Strasbourg. The first of them, Armand Gaston, natural son of Louis XIV and described by St. Simon as the "most handsome prelate of the Sacré Collège" initiated the construction of a new episcopal palace in a town whose reattachment to France in 1681 also marked the return to the Catholic religion. Being a secular leader as well as prince of the church, the prelate wanted a prestigious palace. The design was entrusted to Robert de Cotte, and the work, begun in 1730, spread over ten years, with the collaboration of artists and

The Palais Rohan, formerly an episcopal residence, now houses three museums.

Palace Rohan,
2, place du Château
Open every day except Tuesdays from 10.00 am to 6.00 pm.
Information: Tel. 0388525000.

The Bishops' Hall at the Palais Rohan.

craftsmen from all over Europe. The episcopal palace takes the form of a vast square construction of yellow and pink sandstone, built around a central courtyard. Its principal entrance opens onto place du Château and is situated practically opposite the south portal of the cathedral. On the other side its harmonious facade, extended by a vast terrace, looks over the Ill. In the centre are four columns of colossal order supporting a pediment and a roof in the form of an imperial-style dome. The iconography of the sculptures varies between the two sides. On the cathedral side, religious and moral motifs dominate. For example, above the large portal we see Faith, represented by a statue carrying a cross and a bible, and Temperance, shown by a child leading a lion. On the Ill side are the secular motifs: the four seasons, the five senses, the heroes and gods of Antiquity, the times of day. One of the most beautiful sculptures, a woman's face with eyes closed, personifying night, is to be found in the chapel to the left of the building. On the facade in the interior of the courtyard can be seen the four corners of the earth and the human temperaments, separated by the figure of a madman in the middle. These grotesque figures found a following, and they may be seen throughout the city on a large number of private buildings from the 18th century .

Louis XV was the first guest in the royal apartments, which were designed on the same lines as Versailles. On that occasion the terrace provided the setting for sumptuous festivities, as it did in honour of Marie-Antoinette. Some years later, however, there was nothing but talk of the "queen's necklace affair", in which the Cardinal was implicated. Bombed in 1870 and then again in 1944, the palace has since regained its former splendour. The apartments include the Synod hall, the bishops' parlour, the king's bedroom and the chapel/library, which can be visited along with the minor apartments – smaller, more comfortable rooms for everyday living. The King's Chamber, or canopy room, is designed precisely according to the style of Versailles. The decor, incorporating mirrors and asymmetric sculptures, is in Rococo style. All the decorative motifs follow a theme of sleep: poppies, flowers of slumber; dragonflies, symbolising dreams; people wearing night-caps surrounded by bats and nocturnal

birds, etc. Another room not to be missed is the library, all in gold and mahogany, the work of the cabinet maker Bernard Kocke. Parallel to the large apartments, looking over the courtyard, are the minor apartments. In one of these, the "morning room", hang portraits of the four Rohans who followed each other onto the episcopal throne between 1704 and 1803: Armand Gaston (1704-49), François Armand (1749-56), Louis-Constantin (1756-79) and finally the "necklace cardinal"

Inkwell by Paul Hannong from around 1750 in the Musée des Arts Décoratifs.

◀ *View of a room in the Musée Archéologique.*

▼ *Showcase containing ceramics in the Musée Archéologique.*

Louis-René-Edouard (1779-1803), who emigrated to Ettenheim after the French Revolution.

But most important of all, the palace houses three extraordinary museums. The **Musée Archéologique** is one of the most important archaeological museums in France and shows Alsace over several millennia, from 600,000 B.C. till 800 A.D., in a very contemporary presentation. In the **Musée des**

La Belle Strasbourgeoise, ▶
by Nicolas de Largillière, at the
Musée des Beaux-Arts.

View of the
Salute from the
Entrance of the
Grand Canal,
by Canaletto,
at the Musée
des Beaux-Arts.

Arts Décoratifs, on the ground floor, can be seen in particular a collection of 18th century ceramics by Hannong, including spectacular trompe l'oeil pieces, as well as the cardinals' apartments in the style of Versailles.

The **Musée des Beaux-Arts** allows a glimpse at the history of painting in Europe from the Middle Ages until 1870 with, notably, works by Giotto, Memling, Boticelli, Raphael, Le Greco, Rubens, Canaletto, Tiepolo, Goya, Corot and Courbet.

The landing stage of the Palais Rohan – situated in place du Marché aux Poissons – is the starting point for tourist boats offering trips on the Ill.

Boat Trips *are possible every day.*
In the summer until late in the evening.
Reservations and Information
Tel.: 03 88 84 13 13, www.batorama.fr

Musée de l'Œuvre Notre-Dame ④

At 3, place du Château twin buildings – one crowned by a crenellated gable from 1347, the other by a scrolled gable from 1585 – bear witness to a harmonious transition between styles. The group is rounded off by the Hôtel du Cerf and a 17th century half-timbered house looking over a Gothic garden arranged according to the instructions of Albert the Great. Together, all these buildings are the home of the Musée de l'Œuvre Notre Dame, which takes its name from the mediaeval foundation in charge of collecting the items necessary for the construction of

A small Gothic garden arranged according to the principles laid down by Albert the Great.

Musée de l'Œuvre Notre-Dame
3, place du Château. Open every day except Mondays
from 10.00 am to 6.00 pm. Information: tél. 0388525000

The Musée de l'Œuvre Notre-Dame with its twin gables, one crenellated and the other scrolled, as a synthesis of Middle Ages and Renaissance.

St. Catherine and St. Madelaine, painting by Conrad Witz at the Musée de l'Œuvre Notre-Dame.

the cathedral. Although it was first intended to house statues from the cathedral, the museum is now dedicated to all types of art from Strasbourg and the Upper Rhine region between the 11th and 17th centuries. The artistic development can be seen in sculptures, paintings, stained glass windows, gold and silver work and tapestries. Also highly recommended are the reconstruction of the Romanesque cloister in Eschau, the original statues from the cathedral portals, sculptures by Nicolas Gerhaert de Leyde and still lifes by Sébastien Stoskopff. The magic of the place remains intact, especially in the former stonemasons' lodge. This guild, still in charge of cathedral maintenance, remains active, but in dif-ferent premises in rue de la Plaine-des-Bouchers.

The Seducer, original sculpture from the 13th century at the Musée de l'Œuvre Notre Dame.

The retable of St. Sébastien at the Musée de l'Œuvre Notre Dame illustrates the end of the Middle Ages.

Rue du Maroquin – Place du Marché-aux-cochons-de-lait ⑤

Rue du Maroquin (Moroccan Street), formerly rue des Cordonniers (Cobblers' Street), is in a perpetual state of activity, due to the great number of restaurants to be found there. But still it would be a shame to miss the view it offers, through a narrow opening, of the Œuvre Notre Dame museum's small Gothic garden. This main pedestrian route leads to place du Marché-aux-cochons-de-lait (Suckling Pig Market Square), whose name is linked to the former Grande Boucherie (Great Slaughter-house), today the Musée Historique, which is situated nearby. The first thing to notice is the large half-timbered corner house adorned with wooden exterior galleries, very rare in town. On the roof of the same building is a weather vane in the form of a boot. This is a reminder of the Emperor Sigismond, who, being dragged to a ball by the ladies of Strasbourg without having had time to put his boots on, stopped here at a cobbler's stall, because his feet were too painful for him to continue his ridiculous journey.

Strasbourg's principal pedestrian zone.

39

Musée Historique ⑥

Situated in the former Great Slaughterhouse dated 1587, the museum offers two important chapters of Strasbourg's history in its new scenographic version, in order to experience again the past in a theatrical light:
- Free City of the Holy Roman-German Empire (1262-1681)
- Free Royal City and Revolution period (1681-1800) which ends with General Kléber's death.
Highlight of the exhibition is the large relief plan dated 1727 and the virtual, highly technological audiovisual show.

The Musée Historique is to be found in the former Great Slaughterhouse of 1586.

The Musée Historique:
every day except Mondays, from 10am to 6pm.
2, rue du Vieux Marché aux Poissons, phone: 03 88 52 50 00.

Cour du Corbeau ⑦

Pont du Corbeau (Raven Bridge), also known as pont des Suppliciés (Bridge of the Condemned), holds sinister memories. It was in this place that, in the Middle Ages, prisoners condemned to death were lowered in iron cages into the waters of the Ill.

Opposite, behind a neutral facade, at 1, quai des Pêcheurs (Fisherman's King of Prussia, in 1740. Also a guest was Gérard de Nerval. He is not mentioned, but his eventful stay in September 1836 is recounted by Alexandre Dumas. The most characteristic section of the buildings, with wooden galleries, circular stair tow-

One of the oldest inns in Strasbourg.

Quay) hides Strasbourg's oldest inn. Mentioned in 1306, it was formerly called "Zum Rappen" (The Stallion), and became known as "Zum Raben" (The Raven). In the paved courtyard, which features a Renaissance fountain in the shade of a large chestnut tree, a copper plaque commemorates the famous guests who stayed here. Among them were the Maréchal de Turenne in 1647, Jean-Casimir, King of Poland, in 1669 and Frederick the Great, er and footbridge, dates from 1632. On the ground floor, behind large wooden doors, are the stalls: space for stables and carriages. From the 18th century until 1854, when it was closed, the hostelry also served as a post station. At the end of the courtyard is a high building with oriel and gable, behind whose wide bay windows was probably the communal room of the inn. The whole building has been just renovated and it is now a hotel.

Musée Alsacien ⑧

If we cross place du Corbeau and take the quai St. Nicolas we come to the Musée Alsacien.

It was created at the end of the 19th century and initially occupied only one of the pretty Renaissance houses along the Ill. Since then, through investment in the neighbouring houses, the museum has been able to spread

The sign of the Musée Alsacien, designed by Paul Braunagel in 1906.

out its treasures more comfortably. This museum of popular art is a collection of items bearing witness to traditional Alsatian life, organised according to precise themes: habitat, furniture, ceremonies relating to the different stages of life, religious and secular imagery. It feels less like a museum than like someone's home: in the kitchen, one expects to see an Alsatian farmer's daughter wiping her hands on her apron. In the parlour, one can imagine that the occupants are simply out at the moment, working in the fields. In addition to these reconstructed interiors, from the wine grower's premises in Ammerschwihr to the cattle farmer's summer hut in the Munster Valley, there are workshops: forge, ropemaker, silk flower maker etc. This is a museum full of character with many secret nooks and crannies, whose waxed wooden floors are best trod at leisure. The Musée Alsacien also houses interesting collections of Catholic, Protestant and Jewish religious art, in particular baptismal blessings or "goettelbrief", elaborately worked according to different techniques.

---

i Information

Musée Alsacien
23, quai St. Nicolas
Open every day except Tuesdays from 10 am to 6 pm.
Information: tel. 0388525001

Wintzenheim's parlour at the Musée Alsacien.

The kitchen at the Musée Alsacien.

Betschdorf ceramics at the Musée Alsacien.

A baptismal blessing from 1863 at the Musée Alsacien.

The wine grower's premises at the Musée Alsacien.

St. Thomas' Church ⑨

Crossing the pont St. Nicolas (St. Nicholas' Bridge), opposite the church of the same name, it is possible to take a pretty stroll along the promenade following the banks of the Ill. All you need to do is take the little staircase opposite the Renaissance house at 1, rue de la Douane, which leads to the quay. From there, follow the bank, and after passing under the pont St. Thomas (St. Thomas' Bridge), listed in the inventory of Historical Monuments as an example of metal architecture

St. Thomas' organ, on which Albert Schweitzer gave numerous concerts.

St. Thomas' church *is open every day.*
Information: tel. 0388321446.

A hall church, whose nave and side aisles are of equal height.

around 1840, you can climb back to the pavement level, to find **St. Thomas' church,** easily recognisable with its huge Romanesque tower. This church, originally founded by Irish monks, was built between the 12th and 15th centuries. The exterior of the church is striking due to its bulky appearance. Its on the west side is a porch-tower dating from 1230. It is decorated by a rose window inspired by the one in the south transept of the cathedral and a Lombardic arcade above sculpted heads in Romanesque style. The church was the first to adopt Protestantism when the town was converted at the time of the Reformation in 1529. Today, it heads the biggest Lutheran parish in Alsace. The interior layout is that of a "hall church", characterised by the equal height of nave and side aisles, ex-

amples of which can also be seen in the Rhineland and the Netherlands. It is a veritable museum of funerary sculpture, with, in particular, the tomb of Bishop Adeloch from the 12th century. Numerous illustrious professors from the University of Strasbourg are buried there, such as Jean-Daniel Schoepflin, Christophe Guillaume Koch and Jérémie Jacques Oberlin. The most famous monument is the mausoleum of the Maréchal de Saxe which decorates the choir. Sculpted entirely in white marble by Jean-Baptiste Pigalle, it is one of the masterpieces of French 18th century statuary. The Maréchal is shown descending majestically into the tomb, surrounded by animals symbolising the nations he conquered during his blitz-like military career in the service of Louis XV. But to fully appreciate the atmosphere of this church, you should attend a concert given on its exceptionally sonorous Silbermann organ. Nobel Peace Prize winner Albert Schweitzer played it frequently when he lived in Strasbourg.

A masterpiece of funerary sculpture: the mausoleum of the Maréchal de Saxe, by Pigalle.

Petite France ⑩

As you come out of St. Thomas' church, rue de la Monnaie, where, until the 18th century, the city of Strasbourg minted its own currency, remains, designating the whole of this former tanners' quarter, which is interwoven with canals.

Rue des Dentelles (Lace Lane),

All traffic on the navigation canal must pass through the lock.

leads via rue des Dentelles to place Benjamin Zix. Here is the heart of **Petite France,** whose name, however, has nothing patriotic about it. In this quarter was a hospital for patients suffering from the "French disease" – syphilis, which was spread at the end of the 15th century by the troops of Franz I. The hospital has since disappeared, but the name

bordered by picturesque houses, but also by the beautiful Hotel des Rathsamhausen, dating from 1587, whose interior courtyard may be admired, was formerly known as Spitzegasse (Pointed Street). In fact it was situated at a bend in the tanners' trench, which fed into the Ill until it was covered up in 1877. The street's poetic name is the result of

One of the most beautiful views of Strasbourg can be seen from the panoramic terrace of the Vauban dam. The view from this side has

changed little over the centuries.

Maison des Tanneurs, former seat of the tanners' guild.

an erroneous translation from German into French. On the banks of the Ill, place Benjamin Zix, shaded by trees, is a good place for admiring the former tanners' houses. The roofs are particularly noticeable for their large openings which aided the airing of the attics or drying-out of the skins. The most remarkable building is called "Maison des Tanneurs" (Tanners' House) and was the seat of the tanners' guild. Another, called "Lohkäs", has an intriguing name. It refers to the little cheeses (käs) of tanin (lohe) which, after being used to prepare the skins for tanning, were collected and used as fuel.

The walk may be continued either along rue du Bain-aux-Plantes or by

The mini-tram goes across the quarter „Petite France", too.

Tourist boats offer trips through Petite France by night as well as by day.

Like Montmartre: painters in place Benjamin Zix.

The cut-away roofs of the houses were formerly used for drying out hides.

In front of the "Petite France" which has to be investigated by canoe...

further following the course of the navigation canal. The latter route involves negotiation of a metal swing bridge, which opens to let tourist boats through. So a little patience is required of pedestrians, who have to wait their turn. But waiting offers an opportunity to admire the cut-out sculptures of the Goethe Foundation, found here. The path continues, past houses in a whole palette of pastel colours reflecting in the water, until the Ponts Couverts (covered bridges), recognisable by four mediaeval towers. These solid square towers are what remains of a former chain of fortifications consisting of over 80 towers in total. Dating from the third extension of the city in around 1230-1250, they gave an indication of the independence enjoyed by Strasbourg while it was a free city of the Germanic Holy Roman Empire. The towers, called Tour du Bourreau, Heinrichsturm, Hans von Altheimturm and Tour des Français, were for many years used as a prison. The bridges, the oldest of the city and formerly fortified in the manner of the Ponte Vecchio in Florence, lost their roofs in the 18th century and were replaced in the 19th century by new freestone bridges. Opposite is the Barrage Vauban (Vauban dam), whose construction was ordered by Louis XIV as soon as Strasbourg had been reattached to France in 1681, as a means of reinforcing the former mediaeval fortifications. In fact it was a lock dam, whose gates could be lowered in order to flood the south side of the city in the event of invasion. Today, the top of this military construction has been converted into a panoramic terrace. From here is a clear view over a district formed into a sort of river delta by four canals: Zornmühle, Dinsenmühle, Spitzmühle and the navigation canal. These names – "mühle" means "mill" – are a reminder that the tanners' neighbours were millers, even though the large mills have since disappeared. Between the canals are pleasantly arranged squares. And the towers of all

Mediaeval towers, a vestige of the chain of fortifications.

the principal churches in Strasbourg are silhouetted against the sky. In the foreground rises the most remarkable of all, St. Pierre-le- Vieux, with its two bell towers, one Catholic, the other Protestant.

The view offered by the other side of the terrace is completely different, consisting of the regional administrative centre, designed by the architect Vasconi, and the museum of modern art, by Adrien Fainsilber,

There is nothing better than a boat tour for getting to know the old town.

with its huge bay windows which are lit as soon as it gets dark. The contemporary silhouettes of both buildings mingle with that of the little bell tower of the former Commanderie St. Jean (now the National School of Administration – École Nationale d'Administration or ENA), thus depicting a huge leap across the centuries.

Musée d'Art Moderne et Contemporain ⑪

Built by the architect Adrien Fainsilber and inaugurated in November 1998, the MAMCS boasts a panoramic terrace which overhangs the Ill and looks over Petite France.

On entering, the visitor is drawn down a large hallway, a veritable indoor highway leading to the different rooms and services such as the boutique bookshop, the auditorium, the library and the café-restaurant. All the great artistic movements of the end of the 19th and first half of the 20th century are represented: pieces by Gauguin, Rossetti, Rodin, Bonnard, Braque, Picasso, Richiez, Kudo and Schönbeck rub shoulders with works from the Fluxus movement and Arte Povera. A large amount of space is devoted to artists of Alsatian origin or who worked in Alsace. The room next to the entrance, with its transparent walls a real display window of the museum, is dedicated to Jean Hans Arp, while a little further on is another room especially designed for the works of Gustave Doré, in particular his monumental painting, "Christ Leaving the Praetorium". In addition, the Musée d'Art Moderne et Contemporain is in possession of an exceptional collection of over 4000 photographs, of which the oldest dates from 1842. The photographs of Eugène Atget form a bridge between the 19th century and the beginning of the modern period.

The main facade of the Musée d'Art Moderne et Contemporain.

Musée d'Art Moderne et Contemporain
1, place Hans-Jean Arp.
Opening times every day except Mondays from 10am to 6 pm.
Information: 0388233131.

Beautifully
sweeping lines at
the Musée d'Art
Moderne et Con-
temporain.

Allegory of
Spring at the
Musée d'Art
Moderne et
Contemporain.

Woman and
Sailing Ship by
Marcelle Cahn at
the Musée d'Art
Moderne et Con-
temporain.

Sculpture by
Hans-Jean Arp at
the Musée d'Art
Moderne et Con-
temporain.

Place de l'Homme de Fer ⑫

Place de l'Homme de Fer, previously without great character, was completely remodelled when the new tram system came into operation. The main function of the great glass rotunda of 700 m^2, which is now a feature, is to proclaim the existence of a tram stop destined to play an increasingly important role. What is more, the square has become an interchange between the different modes of transport, bringing together in one place bus-stops and taxi points and constituting a sort of anti-chamber to the pedestrian zone. The iron man who gives the square its name is still in place: on a pharmacy sign depicting a man in a 17th century suit of armour. In fact, until 1681, at the sound of the tocsin all the members of the Strasbourg guilds had to present themselves, thus armed from head to foot, in front of the cathedral, ready to defend the city against a potential enemy. The current Man of Iron is a 19th century copy of the original, which is preserved in the Musée Historique.

The Rotunda has become emblematic of place de l'Homme de Fer.

Place Kléber

Renovated and enlarged, place Kléber constitutes more than ever the heart of the city. Modern street lamps stand alongside freshly-planted trees. The statue of General Kléber, native of Strasbourg, has been enthroned on its pedestal since occupied the major part of the site. This was at the time when the square was known as place des Déchaussés (literally "Square of the Unshod"). In the 18th century it became known as place d'Armes when military marches took the place of religious

A very contemporary tram system in front of the 18th century Aubette.

1840 and a whole squadron of flags stand on parade. The square is the main forum for public entertainment and always the centre of festivities. In the Middle Ages a large church attached to a Franciscan monastery, dedicated to St. Francis of Assisi, chanting and processions gave way to military parades. The Aubette, built by Jean-François Blondel, was so named because it was designed to house the Corps de Garde, who always received their orders at dawn (aube). After the siege of 1870, the

59

building, converted into an academy of music, was restored and decorated with medallions commemorating musicians such as Mozart, Gluck and Handel, which can still be seen today. Next, the building was turned into a restaurant. The interior design was entrusted to Jean Arp, another son of the city, his wife, Sophie Taeuber, and Théo Van Doesburg. The idea was to create a daring leisure complex consisting of tea rooms, cinema, ballroom, billiard room, nightclub etc. The "Ciné-Bal", classed as a historical monument, has just been restored.

Not to be overlooked, Place Kléber...

...and its constant bustle.

Place Gutenberg ⑭

Every week bookstalls are set up around the base of the statue of Gutenberg, which was erected in 1840. The city does indeed owe him a statue. It was within its walls that he invented the principle of printing with moveable metal characters. At the time he was just a young aristocrat exiled from Mainz, weighed

And there was light!

down by financial worries and possessing a dubious curiosity. In 1445, however, appeared the first bible printed by him. The statue of Gutenberg was created by the sculptor David d'Angers, a renowned artist of the Romantic period. When it was set up, the festivities lasted three days, during which the Strasbourg guilds paraded past in full costume. It is worth taking the time to look at four panels at the pedestal of the statue, which represent the benefits brought to the world by printing. Who would imagine the agitation provoked by the panels devoted to Europe? In fact, the artist had wanted to depict, among other famous people, Luther and Bossuet. In the face of protests from Catholics and Protestants, he replaced them with Erasmus and Montesquieu, two champions of tolerance. The invention of the printing press contributed to Strasbourg's prosperity. Throughout the 15th and 16th century the city was one of the capitals of publishing and played a determining role in the propagation of the ideas of the Reformation. The countless books printed on Strasbourg presses were often remarkably illustrated by artists as famous as Hans Baldung-Grien, whose paintings can be viewed at the Musée de l'Œuvre Notre-Dame.

Book market at the foot of the statue of Gutenberg.

Also in the square, and contemporary to this intense intellectual and artistic activity, is a superb Renaissance building. It was built in 1585 by Hans Schoch and is typical of Alsatian art: an original blend of diverse influences. Although its facade is decorated with antique colonnades, its sloping roof with its many dormers remains faithful to local tradition. The result of this daring enterprise is one of the most elegant 16th century buildings in Alsace. At the time it presented a much more cheerful view than today, since, following the taste of the period, its walls were covered in allegorical frescos in vivid colours. After having been the town hall, notably at the time of the Revolution, when it was plundered, this building is now home to the Chamber of Commerce and Industry of Strasbourg and the Bas-Rhin region. Exhibitions are frequently organised in the vaulted rooms on the ground floor.

The square is linked to the cathedral by rue Mercière with its half-timbered houses, such as nos. 2 and 4. Also noteworthy is no. 8, which boasts a superb 18th century wrought iron balcony.

Rue des Hallebardes

Rue des Hallebardes (Halberd Street) was originally the praetorian route through the Roman military settlement which evolved into Strasbourg. Today, halberds on the facades of buildings recall the

armourers who settled here in the Middle Ages. At no. 5 a beautifully sculptured oriel from 1654 has been remounted on the facade of a building destroyed during the last war. The most remarkable 18th century facades in this street can be found at nos. 7, 8, 12, 13 and 16. But it is at no. 22 that you can find one of the oldest exposed beam Renaissance houses in the city, as attested by the date – 1528 – inscribed on the corner console.

Rue du Dôme

Formerly the principle road through the military settlement, rue du Dôme (Cathedral Street) is today a pedestrian artery bordered by interesting 18th century houses which used to belong to the canons of the Great Chapter of the cathedral. The most imposing is no. 8, Livio House, named after a former mayor of Strasbourg and surrounded by a courtyard and garden. At no. 12 is a building belonging to the Great Choir of the cathedral, which was home to Hans Baldung-Grien and visited by Voltaire. In 1764 its facade was redone according to the taste of the time: sculpted grotesque figures on the ground floor represent two women, one with a lamb, the other with a cockerel. Together, the pedestrian streets around the cathedral form the "golden square" of Strasbourg commerce, often the site of special events.

◀ *Opposite the cathedral:
rue Mercière.*

*A busy pedestrian zone:
one of the streets in the
"golden square".*

Place Broglie ⑮

This area, used in the Middle Ages for equestrian tournaments, was a rough piece of land in 1730, when the military governor in Strasbourg decided to do something with it. François-Marie, Duc de Broglie, one of the best generals of Louis XV, could not put up with the view from the prestigious Hanau-Lichtenberg House, now the town hall, which house, destroyed by fire in 1800, was replaced 20 years later by the present building with its peristyle decorated with muses. Inside, a hall "à l'italienne" with seats of crimson velvet now hosts performances by the Opéra du Rhin. In front of the opera house is an obelisk dedicated to General Leclerc, who, at the head of the 2nd Armoured Division, liber-

Sculptures of the nine muses top the principal facade of the Strasbourg opera house.

was built there. A new promenade was created, where well-dressed ladies vied with soldiers in uniform to be the most elegant. The first opera ated Strasbourg on 23rd November 1944. Nearby an elongated building, fronted by a series of canons, houses the officers' mess. Next to that is a statue of General Kellermann, a native of Strasbourg. A little further on, the facade of the Banque de France is adorned with two medallions. One shows Rouget de Lisle, a Lieutenant in the Rhine Army, who first performed the Marseillaise – the French national anthem – in the salon of the mayor, de Dietrich, on 26th April 1792. The song spread to numerous regiments, including a battalion of volunteers from Marseille. This battalion introduced the song in Paris, which is how it gained the name under which it became famous. Mayor de Dietrich, on the other hand, came under suspicion during the Reign of Terror and was condemned to death at the guillotine in 1793. The other medallion is in memory of Charles de Foucauld, who was born at that place in 1858.

The town hall, former residence of the Hanau-Lichtenberg family.

In December, the square welcomes the "Christkindelsmärik" or Christmas market, where serried ranks of stalls offer tinsel, baubles, Christmas trees and confectionery in preparation for Christmas.

In front of the opera house, the obelisk and statue of General Leclerc.

Place de la République

With its well-trimmed yews, orderly flower beds and straight paths leading to the Monument of the Departed, place de la République has the feel of a French garden. But the buildings which surround it recall Leipzig, Berlin or Vienna. These neo-Renaissance giants, pastiches of Italian palaces, were fashionable during the reign of Emperors William I and Franz

Aerial view of place de la République, where the Palais du Rhin faces the library and the theatre, two national institutions.

The Palais du Rhin was inaugurated in 1889.

Josef. Strasbourg, which was annexed in 1870 and made capital of the Reichsland of Alsace-Lorraine, had to set an example. At the end of the 19th century it took less than 20 years to fill the city with buildings in pure Wilhelmian style. Place de la République had its role to play: as the imperial square it had to be the most prestigious of all, surrounded by buildings which would house the instruments of the new power. It also served as a junction between the old town, nestled between the arms of the Ill, and the new, spread over more than 400 hectares to the north-east of the centre. Five buildings surround the square. The most impressive is the Palais du Rhin, which faces the Strasbourg National and University Library and the building occupied by

the National Theatre, former seat of the regional parliament of Alsace-Lorraine.

The **Strasbourg National and University Library** – or BNUS – collects rarities. It is the only institution in France to be designated both National and University Library. With more than 3 million volumes, it is second only to Paris, and is richly endowed with special resources. Its setting, too, a neo-Renaissance palace, a pastiche of Venetian style, is unusual. It was in 1895 that the "Kaiserliche Universitäts- und Landesbibliothek" was installed in the square, in a new building by two Leipzig architects, August Hartel and Skjold Neckelmann. On the facade is a ring of medallions where Gottfried de Strasbourg is to be found alongside Molière and Shakespeare. A glass dome crowns the central part of the building, under which a reading room with 80 places, surrounded by galleries, has the atmosphere of a cathedral.

The **Palais du Rhin** is a giant in yellow sandstone, a mixture of antique, Renaissance and baroque art, which was specially built for Emperor William I. "Elephantine" is said to have been the imperial reaction on seeing the project by the young Prussian architect, Hermann Eggert. But William I never had the opportunity to stay there. In fact he died in 1888, just as the work was completed, and it was his grandson, William II, who came with great pomp the following year to inaugurate the imperial palace. In this astonishing construction, the decor of the past has retained a great deal of its splendour. The monumental entrance is breathtaking

Ephemeral splendour: the magnolias in bloom.

with its three flights of steps, its fountains of orange marble and its sparkling frescos. This theatrical decor bathes in the frail light from the stained glass windows, which only come to life in the sunlight. The building is home to the Cultural Affairs' Services and the Commission on Rhineland Navigation. It is not open to the public, with the exception of the entrance hall and, in special cases, the reception room.

One either side of the Avenue de la Paix are twin buildings, now containing the Public Treasury and the Prefecture. This point affords a magnificent view of the cathedral.

In the centre of the square, the Monument to the Departed, from 1936, depicts a mother with her two sons: one killed fighting for France, the other killed fighting for Germany.

The Tomi Ungerer Museum – International Centre of the Illustration.

Tomi Ungerer, an artist of worldwide renown, was born in Strasbourg in 1931 and he began his carrier in New York in 1957.

The Tomi Ungerer collection is the result of various donations by the Strasbourg drawer and illustrator to his native city from 1975. It includes 8000 original drawings and prints as well as an important documentation on Ungerer and the illustration arts. Moreover, 6000 toys and games of the artist's personal collection can be admired, too.

«Mine de Rien » („As if it were nothing"), 1980 Pencil and green Indian ink on tracing paper © Museums of the City of Strasbourg / Tomi Ungerer
Photo: Mathieu Bertola

Villa Greiner, 2 av. de la Marseillaise, 67000 Strasbourg.
Tel. 0369063727.
Open every day except Tuesdays from 10am to 6 pm.

St. Paul's Church ⑰

After the University Bridge, the Ill divides into two, forming the Ile Ste. Hélène in the middle. From this piece of land rises majestically St. Paul's church. The neo-Gothic architecture of this building, constructed by Salomon between 1889 and 1892, was inspired by St. Elizabeth's cathedral in Marburg. At the beginning it served as a Protestant place of worship for the German military garrison, before becoming, in 1918, the parish church of the reformed community of Alsace-Lorraine.

St. Paul's: an exceptional site for a neo-Gothic church built in 1889 for the military garrison.

Palais Universitaire ⑱

Among all the examples of German architecture from the end of the 19th century, the Palais Universitaire, built in 1884 by an architect from Karlsruhe, Otto Warth, is one of the most harmonious. The outside of the building, fronted by a large staircase and punctuated by columns, was inspired by the Genoese palaces of the Italian Renaissance. Round the yellow sandstone facade are portrayed famous people from Leibniz to Kant. Inside, a glass roof lets in a zenithal light over a vast marble hall, bordered by a gallery which was once painted Pompey red. But the Palais Universitaire is only the figurehead of a vast collection of institutes built around a garden of eight hectares. Over the years, its beautiful ordered arrangement had given way to anarchic vegetation, until a recent restoration returned it to its former splendour and transformed it into a place for peaceful strolls, in keeping with the studious nature of the place. While most of

One of the most famous students of the University of Strasbourg; Johann Wolfgang Goethe.

ⓘ **The Planetarium:** *„cosmic cinema", open every day.*
The Great Dome of the Observatory
In a setting worthy of Jules Verne, the optical and mechanical workings of the equatorial telescope are presented in night-time sessions observing stars and planets.
Information: Tel.: 03 68 85 24 50
Zoological Museum: *29, boulevard de la Victoire*
Open every day except Tuesdays from 10am to 6 pm.
Information: tel. 0368850485

The university gardens surrounding the building offer one of the most pleasant walks of the city.

the institutes remain solely devoted to teaching and research, the Zoological Museum, the Scientific Gallery, the Museum of Seismology, the Great Dome of the Observatory and the Planetarium are, like the gardens, open to the public and are a first step towards the creation of a Garden of Sciences, a link between the city and the university.

Musée Zoologique

Here, the visitor may discover landscapes as varied as the polar regions and the banks of Lake Tanganyika and rare or extinct animals; he is shown the richness of Alsatian wildlife, may wander through the new insect gallery or relive the history of the museum, thanks to the natural history presentation by Jean Hermann, the museum's founder. Temporary exhibitions, a nature library and science discovery workshops for young people add to the attractions of this museum.

At the Musée Zoologique: displays to stimulate curiosity.

Place St. Etienne ⑲

So-called since the 13th century, place St. Etienne is another of Strasbourg's charming little squares, constantly bustling with school children and students. Many of them are headed for the large Renaissance building in the square, crowned with an ornately scrolled gable. Until the French Revolution it was the seat of the directorate of aristocrats of the Basse-Alsace region. Today it is home to the FEC (Catholic Students' Foyer).

In the middle of the square, under the shade of a large plane tree, can be seen the graceful figure of the "Charmeur de Mésanges" or Flute Charmer. This statue was offered in 1931 by the city of Munich in exchange for a huge Father Rhine figure which sat in state in front of the opera house in place Broglie. Around the square most of the houses have architectural characteristics which attract attention. No. 7, a summary of all the styles from the 16th to the 18th century, is decorated with carved heads wearing attributes of music and science. The building named "Zum Himmelreich" (to the kingdom of heaven) has given its name to the adjoining Rue de Ciel (Heaven Street), just as no. 10, formerly Maison de l'Arc-en-Ciel (Rainbow House) gave its name to the next street. From place St. Etienne, rue des Frères leads to the cathedral, passing the large 18th century seminary which houses a richly-stocked library (visits only for groups, and by appointment).

The charming flute charmer, originally from Munich.

The European Quarter

The European quarter is found in the north of Strasbourg, where the Ill meets the Marne-Rhine Canal. Families of black and white swans swim peacefully at the foot of great buildings in a very contemporary architectural style, home to the European institutions. There are more and the countries belonging to the Council of Europe are permanently raised. Inside, the building surrounds a vast parliamentary chamber (the Hemicyle) and private gardens. It is the seat

The Palais de l'Europe, built by Henri Bernard, Grand Prix de Rome winner, in 1975.

more of these institutions in Strasbourg, which shares with New York and Geneva the privilege of welcoming the headquarters of international organisations without being a state capital.

The **Palais de l'Europe** ⑳ is immediately recognisable. It is an imposing quadrilateral of pink sandstone, glass and steel, which was built in 1975. In its forecourt, the flags of all of the Council of Europe, created in 1949. The Council was the first international parliamentary assembly in history, and its objective is to achieve a closer union between European states respecting Human Rights.

In 1958 Strasbourg was chosen as the meeting point of the Assembly of the European Community, today known as the European Parliament and elected by universal suffrage.

The building of the European Parliament is reflected on the river Ill.

In 1992 at the Edinburgh Summit, Strasbourg also became the permanent seat of the **European Parliament.** ㉑ This decision entailed the construction of a new parliamentary chamber, since, up to now, both the Council of Europe and the Parliament had used the one in the Palais de l'Europe. Entrusted to the company Architecture Studio, who participated in the creation of the Institute of the Arab World, it was completed in 1998. The building, with its majestic curved facade, which traces for half a kilometre the banks of the Ill and of the Marne-Rhine canal, and its reflective tower, whose summit mirrors the image of the cathedral, has managed to avoid the trap of monumentalism, thanks to a complex yet articulate form of expression which constantly throws back to Galileo's circle fig-

ures and Kepler's ellipse. Built on a 200,000m^2 site, the complex consists of six distinct areas, which are, however, linked under a common roof and interspersed with walkways, gardens and footbridges. The heart of the building, where official debates and the voting ceremony take place, is the 750-seat chamber, topped by an instantly recognisable oaken dome of 8000m^2. The dome swells out of a great arc-shaped building, which contains the meeting rooms. This is next to the large 60m tower housing 1133 offices. Other spaces are used for meetings, a press centre, a restaurant, receptions and so on.

In addition, the Members of Parliament have the use of four buildings built especially for them. Constructed as an extension of the Council of Europe, these dark-coloured build-

Aerial view of the quarter where all the European institutions are to be found. On the left, the European Parliament and the other parliamen-

Parlement: ARCHITECTURE STUDIO

tary buildings; on the right, the Palais de l'Europe and the Palais des Droits de l'Homme. (Human Rights Building).

79

ings are known as I.P.E. (Immeubles du Parlement Européen or European Parliament Buildings).

Strasbourg is also the seat of the European Court of Human Rights. Each individual who is a victim of an act incompatible with the European Convention on Human Rights can take his case before this court. But first of all it is necessary to have exhausted all other avenues on the national level, and to belong to a European Union country which has ratified the Convention. A new

Human Rights Building ㉒ was inaugurated in 1995. Its architect was Richard Rogers, who designed the Lloyds Bank building in London and was jointly responsible for the Centre Beaubourg in Paris. He imagined the new building: *"like a ship following the lines of the water. Around the two towers of pink Vosges sandstone which house the plenary sessions of the European Court of Human Rights, the exterior of the liner is as airy as possible, thanks to a blend of translucent glass and metal panels"*.

The Human Rights Building: like a ship following the course of the water.

Parc de l'Orangerie

Lovers go boating on the lake, children delight in the zoo and the parliamentarians come here to clear their heads between two sessions. A few paces from the Palais de l'Europe, the Orangery Park is still Strasbourg's largest and most frequented haven of greenness. Tradition has it that its avenues were designed by Le Nôtre immediately after Strasbourg rejoined France in 1681. In 1807 an elegant pavilion was built there to provide shelter for one hundred orange trees, presented by Louis X of Hesse-Darmstadt to the city of Strasbourg. Two years later, sumptuous banquets were held in honour of the visit of the Empress Josephine. But it was not until the following century, on the occasion of the Exhibition of Industry and Commerce organised in 1895, that the park was substantially modified and an Alsatian farm was transplanted from Molsheim. It is still there, and, under the name of "Buerehiesel", contains a renowned restaurant. The artificial lake and the zoo also date from this period. Since then, other attractions have been introduced, among them bowling lanes and a skateboard area. But the park has lost nothing of its charm, with its romantic paths, rose garden and sometimes surprising sculptures, like the "Red Moon", seen only by the curious leaning to look over the rim of a well.

Romantic pavilion in the Parc de l'Orangerie.

A haven of peace in the heart of the city.

Strasbourg and Alsatian specialities

The colourful world of pottery

Most often suggested as a souvenir is a piece of pottery. The most popular comes from Betschdorf and Soufflenheim, two villages about 30 km north of Strasbourg, where the crafts-people carry out their work according to ancestral methods. All the varieties of these two pottery styles are to be found throughout Strasbourg.

The Betschdorf pottery can be recognised by its grey background decorated with cobalt blue motifs. Its glaze is achieved by adding salts during the firing, which takes place at a very high temperature (1300°). This particularly delicate technique requires a perfect mastery of the clay and the fire. The Betschdorf pottery includes pretty little jugs for white wine, like those which adorn the tables in wine bars, but also beer tankards, vinegar bottles and pots of all sizes: for mustard, lard, eggs, sauerkraut, etc. The pottery from Soufflenheim is more colourful. The turned or moulded forms are decorated, as a baker would decorate a biscuit, with the help of a "barolet" or quill box – a clay receptacle for the glaze, topped with a goose feather. The colours are made from a base of clay, water and metal oxides, which offer a wide range of nuances. As for the motifs, they are generally of naive inspiration, and themes involving the heart, marguerites, birds, are well represented. The Soufflenheim pottery includes numerous traditional pieces, such as moulds for the kougelhopf cake or dishes for baeckeoffe, a mixed-meat casserole. Historical pieces are also available, a little antiquated, but brought up to date, such as comb holders, spoon holders, flan dishes, as well as miniature crockery and toys.

Betschdorf pottery.

Soufflenheim pottery.

A sophisticated craft

Under the heading of "artistic souvenirs", one might choose a marvellous piece of marquetry art showing an Alsatian village or landscape. Marquetry, which was previously confined to cabinet making, was elevated to the rank of an art form in its own right by Charles Spindler during the 1900s. Today, his successors carry out this delicate work, which uses woods of different types to recreate finely and precisely the smallest details of a pre-drawn design.

Or maybe you would prefer a glass painting with bright colours and naive decoration, a style which once had place of honour in every Alsatian parlour. This type of painting, which originated from Bohemia, was most popular between 1750 and 1850. Today, talented artists have rekindled its appeal.

To slip into your suitcase

A colourful piece of furniture, on the other hand, however typical, would rather weigh down the visitor's luggage. Perhaps, in order to take back an example of this type of painted wood art, one must be content with a brightly decorated box, clogs, or wooden toys.

"Textile souvenirs" also take up little space in the luggage. Many tablecloths, handkerchiefs and scarves are decorated with motifs taken from local folklore or inspired by ancient tales. The most well known are the "Hansi" tablecloths and those with a Paisley pattern.

Some weavers have taken to manufacturing "kelch" – a sort of tartan woven using yarns of different colours, predominantly red and blue.

Clog making – a dying profession.

Gastronomic Information

The best foie gras is eaten on the spot. The most renowned is the paté de foie gras en croute, prepared according to the recipe invented by Jean-Pierre Clause, chef of the Maréchal de Contades in the 18th century.

To follow, there is of course sauerkraut, prepared in numerous ways, with fish, à la Juive, etc. But baeckeoffe, a delicious pork, mutton and beef casserole originally cooked in the baker's oven – hence the name, which means just that – is a muchloved alternative. Other dishes of honour in Strasbourg restaurants include coq au Riesling, jugged hare or stuffed pig's stomach. For the fish fans, matelote – a dish where eel, pike, carp, tench and perch are served side by side – is a good recommendation, or perch accompanied by a plate of spaetzle – home-made pasta – and topped with a Riesling sauce. As for the cheese, there is no hesitation: the pungent Munster with or without cumin remains the most characteristic. Another choice for dessert is tarte aux fruits, with a special leaning towards quetsch plums, should they be in season, or cheesecake. But you might also have a "petit faim" – room for just a snack – which can be satisfied in one of the "winstube" – convivial bars which are not to be missed by those who really want to experience

Sauerkraut, a classic of Alsatian cuisine.

The indescribable foie gras.

Strasbourg life.

Here, the main object is to sample the Alsatian wines, each named after the grape variety from which it was made: Riesling, Gewurztraminer, Pinot, Sylvaner, etc. served in a jug.

To accompany them, the winstub menus propose a wide range of snacks, often based on pork, like waedele (pork knuckles), pork riblets, presskopf, tête de cochon or "maennerstolz" (literally "men's pride"), which is a large sausage.

But there are also other specialities, like onion tart, gruyère salad or soft cheese. Finally, more and more restaurants serve, particularly at the weekend, "tarte flambée". This is a very simple dish made from cream, bacon cubes and onions, which was traditionally made on bread-making day, to use up the leftover dough. Tarte flambée is served in the form of a large thin pizza, which may be shared between a few people. The sections are rolled up and eaten, thus eliminating the need for a knife and fork. This meal, which originated in the country, is now also a favourite with city dwellers.

There is nothing better than a tarte aux quetsches.

Christmas in Strasbourg

Over the last few years Strasbourg has been promoted as the Christmas capital, and the city celebrates throughout December. In fact, all aspects of the mediaeval tradition of the Christmas market, for a long time contained within a defined of Christmas delicacies. For a large part of the festivities are devoted to food and to the specialities of the season, from the "maennele" of St. Nicholas to the "stolle" of New Year's day. Guides from the Tourist Office recall Christmas traditions,

Everything for the preparation of Christmas.

area, have disappeared. Today, instead of one Christmas market, there are several, as well as various events throughout the city. The route runs from the station to place de la Cathédrale via all the city's squares. Crib scenes, open-air ice skating, a giant Christmas tree, theatre, concerts are sprinkled along the route, and the air is filled with the smell of cinnamon, of mulled wine and and in particular St. Nicholas' fair, ancestor of today's Christmas markets. That was in the Middle Ages, when the market was established at the foot of the cathedral. Various craftsmen, potters, wood turners and locksmiths showed their skills. In the 15th century the Reformation nearly sounded the death knell for this far too Catholic market. It survived, however, by changing its

An illuminated ring of little stalls at the Christmas market.

name. From St. Nicholas, it became the "Christkindelsmärik" – literally "fair of the Infant Jesus". This is perhaps reminiscent of St. Lucie of the Scandinavian countries. In Alsace, the Infant Jesus is represented by a young girl dressed in white and crowned with candles. Under its new name, the market did not cease to prosper. In the 18th century it became a cosmopolitan event where the Périgord truffle jostled for space with the Bavarian clay pipe. In 1830 the market established itself in place Kléber. The picturesque mediaeval booths had given way to military rows of stalls "like houses in a town fortified by Vauban". Finally, in 1870, the Christkindelsmärik took up its current place in place Broglie. At that time it was entirely dedicated to the preparations for Christmas: the decoration of the Christmas tree, as well as the presents displayed underneath it. While it has not lost that aspect today, the market's palette of traditional products has been considerably enriched by the presence of numerous craftspeople from all over France and from abroad. And, from place Broglie, the stalls have

once more with mediaeval tradition. This event has become so popular that it has made December into the busiest month of the tourist year.

The quayside made white by winter.

Information

Practical Information

Administration

City of Strasbourg
Administrative Centre - 1, Parc de
l'Etoile tel. 03 88 60 90 90,
www.strasbourg.eu

Palais de l'Europe
Council of Europe tel. 03 88 41 20 29
hub.coe.int
(group visits)

European Parliament: tel. 03 88 17 20 07

Chamber of Commerce
www.strasbourg.cci.fr
10, place Gutenberg tel. 03 88 75 25 25

Main Post Office
5, avenue de la Marseillaise
tel. 03 88 52 35 50 www.laposte.fr

Accomodation

Youth Hostel Des deux Rives
Parc du Rhin, rue des Cavaliers
tel. 03 88 45 54 20

Campsites

**Terrain de camping et de caravaning
de la Montagne-Verte**
rue Robert Forrer (entrance rue du
Schnokeloch) tel. 03 88 30 25 46

Tourism

Tourist Information Office for Strasbourg and the Surrounding Area.
Tourist Information Office : 17, place de
la Cathédrale - tel. 03 88 52 28 28 ,
www.otstrasbourg.fr Place de la Gare :
tel. 03 88 32 51 49

**Regional Tourist Information Office of
the Bas-Rhin Region.**
www.tourisme67.com, 9, rue du Dôme
tel. 03 88 15 45 80

**Regional Office for Rural Tourism –
gîtes de France,**
www.gites-de-france-alsace.com
4, rue Bartisch, phone: 03 88 75 56 50

Transport

Taxis
tel. 03 88 75 19 19 or 03 88 36 13 13

**Strasbourg – Entzheim International
Airport,** www.strasbourg.aeroport.fr
tel. 03 88 64 67 67

SNCF : Trains, information and bookings: tel. 36 35, www.sncf.com

Strasbourg Transport Company (CTS)
- (Buses and Trams)
14, rue de la Gare aux marchandises
Allo CTS Service: 03 88 77 70 70 - minitrams tel. 03 88 77 70 03

Batorama (tourist boat trips)
15, rue de Nantes - tel. 03 88 84 13 13,
www.batorama.fr

Parkings: www.parcus.com

Place des Halles(P2) : 24h/24 – 7/7

Sainte -Aurélie : 24h/24 – 7/7

Sainte - Marguerite - Petite France : variable opening times.

Opéra Broglie : 24h/24 – 7/7

Gutenberg : 24h/24 – 7/7

Austerlitz : 7am/2am Mondays-Saturdays
10am/2am Sundays and Bank Holidays.

Bateliers : 7am/2am Mondays-Saturdays.
Closed on Sundays and Bank Holidays.

Kléber : 24h/24

Key to the street plan

① Place de la Cathédrale

② The cathedral

③ The Palais Rohan

④ Musée de l'Œuvre Notre-Dame

⑤ Rue du Maroquin – Place du Marché-aux-Cochons-de-Lait

⑥ Musée Historique of the city

⑦ Cour du Corbeau

⑧ Musée Alsacien

⑨ St. Thomas' Church

⑩ Petite France

⑪ Musée d'Art Moderne

⑫ Place de l'Homme de Fer Place Kléber

⑬ Place Gutenberg

⑭ Place Broglie

⑮ Place de la République

⑯ St. Paul's Church

⑰ Palais Universitaire

⑱ Place Saint-Etienne

⑲

⑳ Palais de l'Europe

㉑ European Parliament

㉒ Human Rights Building

 Tourist Information

 Public Toilets

 Taxi

 Telephone

▬▬▬ **Recommended circuit through the old town**

▬ ▬ ▬ **Recommended route to the "Ville Allemande" (German town)**

The street plan was based on aerial photographs by AIRDIASOL, Roger Rothan.